Occupying Nazareth

Copyright © 2025 by Myrtle Hedge Press, Kure Beach NC
All rights reserved
Printed in the United States of America

ISBN: 978-1-7329970-5-9
Library of Congress Control Number:

Design and layout by
    Val Sherer, Personalized Publishing Services
ID 304294869 © Andrii Lomako | Dreamstime.com

No part of this book may be used, reproduced, or transmitted in any form or by any means, electronic or mechanical, including photocopying, recording or by any information storage and retrieval system, without written permission from the author, except in the case of brief quotations embodied in critical articles and reviews.

Occupying Nazareth

Mattie McClane

MYRTLE HEDGE PRESS

I.

It was a time
of would-be autocrats
bought lawmakers
and hesitant men
the only votes
that seemed
to count
or to matter
were for local offices
total tallies
for municipal
candidates
with the vision
to look ahead.
This was true
in Nazareth, Ohio
in the year 2030.

There was a party election night
balloons
and confetti filled
the grand hall
the half-circular lobby
of a defunct paper
company
the smells of wet
pulp still rose
from the plastered
walls broken
in places
making unique designs.
The sturdy people gathered
the light of hope
in their eyes. Horace Bain
made promises
vowed

restaurants
would come back
after the jobs
and wages
would be
higher than ever before.
Industries
would be taxed
roads repaved.
They called it train town.
Now it was Horace
Bain's town
with the whistles
blowing out
warnings
to the younger set
see the elders'
unfulfilled dreams

the pool
that took what talent
there was
in a land
of little opportunity.

Bain presented
a plan
for renewal
advertised
the town online
in pamphlets
in classifieds
on the East Coast
on the West Coast
where extreme conditions
the mighty
hurricanes sent

rolling balls
of palm
fronds
and wildfires
grew in numbers.
"Come live
in train town
and put weather
worries down."
Citizens elected
him mayor.
Could he deliver
a mass migration?

Days after
the victory
gathering
he drove through

the city alone
to find
three rusty
and abandoned cranes
that looked
like a tall bunch
of blighted
bananas.
The parking lots
where buildings
once stood
went on
for miles
along the one-ways.
Horace had raised
expectations.
Suppose few
responded

to his invitation?
Suppose
he would be
a laughingstock
in his own hometown?
The prairie winds
were fierce
in April. Trees
swayed like dancers
hearing
a swift tempo.
All he could see
was defeat
yet imagining
victory
as his car
shimmied
jiggled

meeting bumps
on the asphalt
patchwork.
What would entice
others to relocate?
he'd sweeten the pot
offer $50,000
per family
to newcomers.

Horace Bain began
a PR campaign
to the town's residents:
"Clean Up Our Town."
mow lawns
trim bushes
and plant trees.
Still there

was a problem:
the homeless
were eyesores
congregating
near churches
and food pantries
in meandering lines
that could thwart
his best ideas
of rejuvenation.
He encouraged
residents
to buy one decent outfit
for video day
when crews
would highlight
the green growing grain
peach sunsets

well-dressed
children.
he would tour
the affluent
neighborhoods
where three-car
garages
were the norm.
By summer,
he was ready
the town
would put its
best footage forward.

In July, prospects
out of towners
began to inquire
about housing

and yearly rainfall
Westerners
wanted to know
if there were any
atmospheric rivers
or dry forests.
Carolinians
expressed relief
that there
were no
torrential rain
events
People were
interested.
People were coming
to where
hundreds
of small framed

houses
dotted the land.
Would these newcomers
be a monied class
be comfortable
in train town's culture?
Horace Bain
dismissed
the question.
locals
desperately
wanted renewal
and seldom
counted a cost.

II. The Mayor

Horace Morris Bain Jr.
followed
his father's
example
and worked
in the shops
just short
of 19.
Ginger
and freckled,
he was a welder whose
protective
apron
with its burnt
pinholes
looked

like stars
in the Milky Way.
he attached
the brakes
on automobiles
steel onto steel
year after year
until the plant
closed down.
Wide empty
storage
buildings
told the story
of workers
with nowhere to go.
Horace took
a class to be
a financial planner.

he worked
at the bank
as a teller
as a loan officer
as a vice president
then ran
for alderman
in the 3rd district
His career
and passions
was beginning
to emerge.
No one would
have guessed
he'd one day be mayor
of the ailing,
rusting,
community.

He had cleaned up
the town
except
for the bleakness
of the wanderers
the homeless
who'd make
their trek
every morning
from the shelter
near the convent
and old fire station:
to the coolness
of the library
on summer
afternoons.

At the convent's door
a heavy
walnut slab
of an entrance
the mayor pleaded
with Sister Frances
to keep
the unfortunates off
the streets
the sidewalks
out of the sight
of coastal visitors.
He explained
the large sum
of money
involved
for each newcomer.

The nun asked,
"Why give
to the newcomer
while some
here are still
suffering?"
He was silent.
He begged
for cooperation.
In his mind,
he answered
her question:
money given
to the poor
never increased.
It was a bad
investment.

He had made promises.
It wasn't cruelty.
It was sound business.

Fall's festivities
filled the calendar
cold beer
hot bratwurst
polka dances
people
were happy
trees turned
to the deep
colors of autumn
maroons
golds
grocery prices
seemed lower.

everyone
was abuzz
with anticipation
of signed contracts
the newcomers
would arrive soon,
early next spring.
This winter
was a time
of preparation,
the hours
to get ready. Train
town stood
to gain a future.

III. The Meeting

The mayor called
December's
council meeting
to order.
Visitors
monied men
said they would
build a wind
turbine plant
if the community
could sustain it.
Dressed lightly
in the midwestern
winter chill,
the below zero
temperature
was more than

the business barons
imagined:
they shivered
when they talked.
Local developers
divided
the farmland
into building sites.
A speculator rose
and suggested
that old
smaller houses
be condemned
quickly razed
to make room
for construction.
newcomers

would need
better housing.

The time came
on the agenda
for citizen's input.
Sister Frances asked
for funding
for 20 new beds
at the homeless shelter.
The honorable mayor
was mortified:
he confronted
the sister
after the meeting.
what was she trying
to do, scuttle

train town's
success? He
had told her
about keeping
the homeless problem
under wraps.
He could not
save them
surely, she agreed.
The sister replied,
"One cannot save
who are unacknowledged.
Won't you
look at them?"
Horace wanted
to tell her
that he saw them
at the grocery store

on the downtown streets
in his dreams.
He could not expect
her, who probably took
a vow of poverty
to understand
his plans
to resurrect train town.

Sister Frances came
close to him
in his space
and gently touched
his forearm. "If you
see them,
then their stories
their lives
and circumstances

would be real,
and you would act."
She told him
there would
be winners
and losers with
any remade
community.

Horace bet
on more winners
than losers
He now read reports
on extreme weather
on homeowner's
insurance
how many coastal
policies

were cancelled
after floods
and wildfires.
weary people
fleeing
to relocate
to the central
states
were his hope.
train town
boasted four
mild seasons
few natural disasters.

The sister seemed
to suggest
that the poor
would be

the losers: the
town was poor
after decades
of industries'
abandonment.
Horace not once
imagined
it could go down
further.

IV. Sister Frances

When the Sisters
of St. Gregory
left town
because people
gave slim offerings
to the Church,
Sr. Frances stayed
behind
to care
for the very poor.
She kept
on her table
a stand-up cross
of Jesus
a warm crust
of bread
and a teacup.

She remembered
the town's
collections' plates
once filled
once heaping
the town bustling
with stores
and eateries.
After the auto plants left,
hucksters came in
there was talk
sham proposals
of the biggest
grandest
theme parks
sports arenas
flashy casinos
to light up

the now dark nights.
Horace was not
the first
to imagine
a restored city:
the others failed.

People were behind
Horace though.
While she
had doubts,
he promised
the clergy would
return, people
would build
new churches
and citizens
would renew

their faith
when they
had a better life.
Horace was a man
with attractive dreams.

In early spring
earthmovers
and demolition
crews began
to appear,
razing small
unpainted
already broken
houses
with displaced
daffodil
now atop

of dirt mounds
of debris like
a conqueror's flag.
For better
or worse,
progress
was everywhere
new buildings
to replace
the old.
Not common homes
but the best
that money
could buy.
People watched
as train town
became
a boom town.

The newcomers
began arriving
moving vans
pulled up
trailers
packed
with belongings
aluminum grills
deck chairs
colorful
sun umbrellas
the train towners
were gleeful
for what looked
so positive.
The new folks
seemed
fashionable

designer
clothing
print
dresses
and leather bags
upscale neighbors.

The privileged
migrants
overtook
overwhelmed
the locals
the disparity
between
the well-off
and the poor
grew. "Train
towners"

became a slur
for the sorry
and downtrodden:
the homeless
numbers
increased
but they
were invisible.
they were not seen
and rarely
spoken of.
The convent
was eventually
torn down.
Sister Frances
moved away,
returning
to the motherhouse

in Akron
where Jesus's
statue
was adored
and glorified.

Horace Bain lost
his bid
for reelection
to a newcomer
a hero
heart was crushed
the light
escaped from
familiar eyes
and he would hear
in his mind
until his dying day:

"Train Town
was Horace
Bain's town
with its whistles
blowing out
warning
to the younger set
see the elders'
unfulfilled dreams
the pool
that took
what talent
there was
in a land
of little opportunity."
Horace fulfilled
his promises.

How odd
it did not go
as he planned.

About The Author

Mattie McClane (Kristine A. Kaiser) is an American novelist, poet, and journalist. She is the second and youngest daughter born to James L. and Shirlie I. Myers in Moline, Illinois. Her father was a commercial artist and her mother worked as a secretary.

McClane's earliest education was in the Catholic schools. Her experience with their teachings deeply affected her. At a young age, she became aware of gender inequality. She credits her early religious instruction for making her think about "all kinds of truths" and ethical matters.

McClane's parents divorced when she was eight years old. Her mother remarried attorney John G. Ames and the new couple moved to a house beside the Rock River. The river centrally figures in McClane's creative imagination. She describes her childhood as being "extraordinarily free and close to nature."

McClane moved to Colorado and married John Kaiser in 1979, in Aurora, just East of Denver.

They then moved to Bettendorf, Iowa where they had three children. John worked as a chemist. Mattie became interested in politics, joining the local League of Women Voters. According to McClane, she spent her 20s "caring for her young children and working for good government."

She graduated from Augustana College with a B.A. degree in the Humanities. She began writing a political column for Quad-Cities Online and Small Newspaper Group, based in Illinois.

Her family moved to Louisville, Kentucky where she continued with her journalism and then earned an M.A. in English from the University of Louisville. Critically acclaimed author Sena Jeter Naslund directed her first creative thesis, "Unbuttoning Light and Other Stories," which was later published in a collection.

She was accepted to the University of North Carolina at Wilmington's M.F.A. in Creative Writing Program, where she wrote the short novel Night Ship, working under the tutelage of Pulitzer Prize winning author Alison Lurie. McClane studied with Dennis Sampson in poetry also. She graduated in 1999.

She would write a column for the High Point Enterprise in North Carolina. She would later write for the News and Observer. McClane has regularly published commentary for over 25 years.

Mattie McClane is the author of *Night Ship: A Voyage of Discovery* (2003), *River Hymn: Essays Evangelical and Political* (2004), *Wen Wilson* (2009), *Unbuttoning Light: The Collected Short Stories of Mattie McClane* (2012), *Now Time* (2013), *Stations of the Cross* (2016), *The Mother Word: An Exploration of the Visual* (2017), and *Simeon's Canticle* (2018), *The Song of the Grackle* (2019), *At the Edge of the Cities Burning* (2023), and *The Tale of the Ancient Haberdasher* (2024).

www.ingramcontent.com/pod-product-compliance
Lightning Source LLC
Chambersburg PA
CBHW050318100526
44585CB00016BA/1725